ɔn or before
d below

THE BELLFIELD RUNNERS

THE BELLFIELD RUNNERS

Alexander B. Taylor

To order additional copies of this book, contact:
Xlibris Corporation
0-800-644-6988
www.xlibrispublishing.co.uk
Orders@xlibrispublishing.co.uk
302355

ACKNOWLEDGEMENTS

A special thanks to:

- My family: May, Scott and Sharon;

- A special thanks to Isabella McGarry for helping the book over the finishing line;

- A special thanks to the BELLFIELD RUNNERS who are no longer with us;

- A special thanks to Enda Ryan, Patricia Grant and Louise Boyle of the MITCHELL LIBRARY, Glasgow for their kindness in supplying the photographs of the Gallowgate, Glasgow;

- Thanks to Lynne Crawford, Archives Department MITCHELL LIBRARY, Glasgow.

THE BELLFIELD RUNNERS

By Alexander B. Taylor

Surfacing from the pile of heavy coats that my mother had covered me with on the previous night to try and keep me that bit warmer in bed, I felt the usual damp coldness of the winter morning and a shiver came over me the moment I stepped onto the bare lino. Rubbing the sleep from my half-closed eyes, I quickly made my way through to the warmth of the living room, where the welcoming glow of the small coal fire made me forget the chills. But still half asleep, I pushed the flimsy lace curtain aside and peered out through the window, which was directly above the kitchen sink, onto the dark street below. To quote an old uncle of mine, it was "Black as the Earl of Hell's waistcoat" out there. The rain was torrential, falling monsoon fashion and assaulting the cobblestones as though it was taking its anger out on them. Underneath the canopy of the yellow glow that filtered out from the streetlights, I could see the spray being lifted from the pools of rainwater as the heavy gusts of wind caught the surface, sending it swirling off in all directions.

The weather had been horrendous over the past few days and had shown no sign of improving. It was a mid-November Friday morning, around half past seven, and here I was walking around like a zombie. It had seemed a waste of time going to bed last night, owing to the cold and the noise that was caused by the shuddering and rattling of the old, well worn wooden window frames, as the wind and rain attacked them with gale force severity, causing a disturbing, creaking and moaning sound that seemed to linger all night long. This was the penance being paid for the luxury of living in an old Glasgow tenement, of post-war Scotland. These same tenements must have been strong and sturdy at one time in the past, but, as most things in the by-gone era, they were allowed to fall into an unforgivable state of disrepair, due to the fact that the people, who owned the properties, were quite happy to receive rent, but not so keen to invest any money towards keeping the houses in good habitable condition. So it was a gradual decline over the years, as the lack of repairs took hold, the buildings became slightly better than slums.

I often found myself letting my memory stray back to that time in my life when I lived in that dilapidated building with my older brother and two sisters in a house that consisted of a living room which was heated by a small coal fire and the lighting came from two gas lamps and the cooking was done on a doubled ringed gas stove which, in the winter, was more often than not kept alight to give some extra heat to the room. There was also the table, four chairs and a chest of drawers, so it was a bit of an obstacle course to move around, as the space was limited. Then there was another room, which could hold two small beds, this is where my brother and I slept. We were quite fortunate, as some families had over seven in their household and they all had to adapt to the same conditions and space, as did the rest of our neighbours. Our family was poor, although it didn't seem so to them, as all the other families were living under the same conditions. This seemed to bring a tighter and closer community together, a type of socialism, in a certain way, where everyone would share what they had, even though it wasn't much but, compared to the materialistic society we live in now, I know the one which I would choose.

Looking back to the morning of the last day of my school year, I can still hear the unbearable staccato drumming sound of the rain as it lashed against the panes seemingly getting louder as the night wore on. After, what had felt like hours, the noise suddenly abated and the wind had died down, "*At* last" I thought, a chance to get a bit of shut-eye, but after lying awake for so long, my mind was too alert and I began to think of all sorts of things, "*Would I be going to the football or the cinema at the weekend, or wait and see what the rest of my pals were thinking of doing?*" Suddenly the worst thought of all sprang to mind, I had a maths exam that very morning and, as this would be my final exams before leaving St. Mungo's for the very last time, and it was really important that I achieved good results, more so as I had reached the end of my final years of schooling and it was now time to take my place alongside the country's working population by finding employment. That was enough to make me, forget how tired I was and start questioning myself, "Could I answer most of the arithmetic problems, enough for a pass mark, would I finish the paper in time, had I studied enough?" With these negative thoughts churning through my mind and tossing and turning for what seemed most of the night, I must have drifted into the all embracing haven of amorphous, because the next thing I recall was my mother standing over me, shaking my shoulder and bringing me back to the land of the living with the unwelcoming words of "C'mon son, it's time to get up for school." Getting out of bed at the ungodly early hours of the morning, particularly at this time of year, never did appeal to me. As far as I was concerned, the darkness was only for the nocturnal characters of the night, like shift workers or the men who came round to empty the backcourt rubbish bins, or the "*middens*" as we called them, but after a quick wash, getting dressed and organised, I felt a bit more comfortable, until I looked out the window and began to shudder, knowing that I had to face that onslaught of weather on my way to school. I sat at the table to have some breakfast, perhaps it had been the lack of sleep or even the thought of the exam looming ahead, because I just didn't feel like eating, so it was a case of a quick cup of tea, coat on, out the door and off to school.

As I left the close mouth and into the street, the cold wind hit me with a vengeance and I was met by a wall of rain that penetrated every part of my clothes and, within a matter of minutes, I was soaked to the skin. There was only one way to get dried out again and that was to get to school as fast as could. Getting to the tram stop meant having to cross the old Bellfield Street railway bridge and then up to Duke Street. I usually took this route and always found it to be really busy, what with people going off to work, or mothers taking their children to school and, with this being a Friday, women with their washing making for the "*steamie*" but, today was different, the place seemed deserted, but the reason soon became clear, approaching the tram stop I noticed that people were cramming into any available space to get out of the rain, into shop doorways, underneath window ledges, I even saw about six women all jockeying for position below one small umbrella, but the thing that really struck me as funny, was to see a group of heads all stretching out of a close mouth watching for a bus. The strange part, as far as I could see, was that they were all gathered in the close trying to keep reasonably warm and dry, and yet here they all had their heads stuck out getting them soaked by the rain, so it's really true "*there's now't as queer as folk.*"

The tram came after a few minutes of me waiting but, as I squelched onto it, a voice from the front seats called out "Hey Alex, down here." It was a classmate of mine, Peter Donnelly. At least things were beginning to look a bit on the up and up as I got on really well with this boy, because there was never a dull moment with Peter around. I got to know Peter three years ago on the first day we both started going to St. Mungo's Academy and it was under the strangest of circumstances that we first met.

After the 11 plus exams at the primary school, I was fortunate enough to obtain the results that allowed me to have a much higher form of education at the Academy, I was really excited at the prospect of being part of this school, as it was one of the elite educational establishments. Yet, here I was with this wonderful opportunity to be part of this famous school. Only the best studied at St. Mungo's. I began to picture myself going on to greater things, the world was my oyster for a few brief moments, then the thought struck me and my fantasies crumbled, there was no way on God's green earth that I could attend this school, the main reason being there was no chance of being able to afford the school uniform which consisted of blazer, trousers, shirt and tie, etc. as my father had died two years previously, leaving my mother to raise my younger sister and myself on a pittance of an income which came largely from family allowance and a small amount of money that my brother James, who was doing his national service, sent home monthly. I was disappointed for a few days, but I soon accepted that going to the Academy was not for me and I would go to the other high school where some of my pals attended. As I was now on my school holidays, it was back to playing football, swimming, playing games and all the usual escapades with my pals, so I soon forgot all about the Academy. I may have thought that I had forgotten about the Academy, but my Mother was determined not to let this opportunity pass. So, for days she had been going about trying to obtain some information on the best way to get me a uniform. As luck would have it, we got a visit from the local priest, Father Murphy, and, as usual, he asked how the family was getting along. After telling Father Murphy how we were coping, my mother mentioned how well I had done in my exams, but things were a bit tight money-wise and how she was trying to get me a uniform. Father Murphy said he would be back in a few days and not to worry as he would see what he could do. True to his word, he was back the following day and gave my Mother a letter with the address of the district parish. This place was a government department which gave assistance to families who were in financial difficulties. So my Mother approached them and told them of the dilemma that she had, in getting a school uniform for me. After answering all types of personal questions and signing all sorts of documents, she eventually got permission to obtain a suit that would allow me to go to the Academy. Even at that young age, I didn't like the embarrassment of going cap in hand for this suit, as it seemed akin to begging, but I soon realised that it must have been worse for my mother, as she was a very proud woman and it went against all her principles to have to ask for this assistance. As for me, even at my young age, I would have been quite happy to tell them where to shove their suit and go to another school. However, my mother was set in her ways and she said I was going to the Academy, at any price. She was then told to go to this corporation department on a Saturday and collect a suit for me. So, on the first available Saturday, off we went. We eventually found the address of the place that supplied the clothes for the less affluent of the city. As we entered the door of this dank, grey run-down building, I felt a shiver running down my spine, I didn't know whether it was the coldness of the place or the atmosphere, the silence and darkness resembled a graveyard. Suddenly, from out of nowhere I caught sight of this old man shuffling towards us. He had a wrinkled, wizened face and wore small pince-nez spectacles that sat on the very tip of his nose, he also had the misfortune to have a prominent facial tic, which caused his head to move sideways whenever his face went into a spasm, and that seemed to be every few seconds. He walked with a very prominent stoop and had the thinnest legs I had ever seen, thankfully in his case they didn't have too heavy a burden to carry, as he resembled a scarecrow. He wore clothing that hung ever so loosely on his skeletal frame and a suit that had seen much better days. Every stitch was doing a fine job, as it appeared that he had been wearing these same clothes since before the war, the first world war that is, and it looked as if he even slept in them. Without even a good morning, his first words were "Name?" after my mother answered with the particulars, he then commanded "Follow me" beckoning us with his large bony finger. As we trailed behind him I couldn't help picturing the way his face contorted and found it very difficult to stop myself from laughing. I guess my Mother knew what was going through my mind, because she gave me a hard dig on the ribs, and a "don't you dare" look. Suddenly, the old bag of bones spun round and before I could stop grinning, he looked over the rim of his spectacles and gave me the "I know what you're thinking" glare and I believe that was my downfall. We went into this large room which had enormous shelves holding all sizes and colours of suits. He then looked me up and down, went to this shelf and took down a suit, to say this thing was a monstrosity, was an understatement. It was a *hairy, brown, herringbone cloth and I would have been more at ease with a boiler suit and then, to add insult to injury, he asked me the size of shoes that I wore, so here was I thinking that I'm going to get a nice pair of shoes—no such luck. He went away and brought back a big pair of brown hob-nailed boots, the soles of which were covered with large steel studs, so that when you walked you sounded like a Clydesdale horse, and if you had to run at any time, sparks came off the studs on the soles, resembling a rocket on Guy Fawkes night. I had never felt so downhearted, knowing that I would have to wear these bizarre clothes on my first day at the new school. So the old rascal got his sweet revenge by giving me a rig-out that made me resemble a country yokel.*

On our way home, my mother must have saw the look of embarrassment on my face, because she turned to me and said that I would only have to wear it for a short while as she was putting some money aside to get me a uniform the same as the other boys. As always, she kept her promise and, for that, I shall be eternally grateful to her.

The day I was dreading arrived and, stepping off the tram and making my way to the school, everywhere I looked there seemed to be boys wearing the school uniform, blazers with the school badge, caps and they all appeared to have leather satchels, whereas I had my hairy suit, brown boots and a brand new pencil clutched in my fist. I realised I must have looked out of place, like a one-legged man at an arse kicking contest, but, to my complete surprise, no one showed the least bit of interest in me, or my outlandish suit. Suddenly, in the crowd of boys all making their way towards the school gates, I had the good fortune to see this boy walking along by himself and "Ye God's' he wore the same type of suit as I was wearing, the only difference being his was a blue herring bone, twice as hairy as mine, and a pair of clodhopper boots similar to the ones I wore. Needless to say, I made a beeline for this boy and started a conversation with him, "where was he from, what school he came from?" I asked all sorts of questions to break the ice and, not be a solitary figure with the type of clothes that I was wearing, we seemed to have the same type of humour and the same interests in all departments. That's how I first met Peter Donnelly and we've been friends ever since that day.

Now here we were, going into our very last exam and both wearing the school uniform. An awful lot of water flowed under the bridge since we first met all those years ago. Suddenly, the rain began to fall heavily, just as we were approaching the school gates. "*Well, here we go me old mucker, this is oor last hurrah, after three years of goin' tae this place together, we'll be leavin' oor learnin' days behind us and in aboot a month frae noo, we'll be oot there lookin' fer a joab, huv ye' gave any thought tae whit kind o'work ye'll be lookin'fer?*" "Ah've nae idea," I said "*but seein' this kind o' weather ah' think ah'll be goin' fer a place in some factory, at least ye'll no be getting' soaked oan days like this.*""*How's this for weather?*" Peter replied, with his usual big infectious grin, "*Tae think there's aw them Arabs and their cronies always moaning it's too warm, get them ower here for a few weeks and I'll bet ye London tae an orange they wid think twice o' pitchin' their tents here.*" "*Tell me aboot it*" I said "*Ah hardly got a wink o' sleep last night, between the rain and the noise o' the wind blawin' ah thought the buildin' wis ready tae collapse aboot me. It's these auld tenements tae blame, Ah widnae be surprised if hauf the roofs in Glesca' had blew aff.*" "*Oor hoose is the very same*" replied Peter "*always cauld even in summer, if and when we get wan. Did ah ever tell ye aboot the time mah maw got the sanitary men in because the hoose wis overrun wi' rats? Well they came intae the hoose and started tae shine their wee torches aw ower the place, in the coal bunker, in the cupboards and even under the beds, puttin' doon traps here and there. then this big chap went tae put wan under the sink, a salmon jumped oot an' nearly took the haun aff him.*" "*Whit the hell wis that?*" he asked, "*Never mind the dampness son*" ma maw replied "*Get rid o' thae bloody rats first.*"

Listening to Peter's absurd tale took my mind off how cold and damp I was and really cheered me up no end. I began to laugh and I couldn't seem to stop, every time I thought about this comical story it would set me off again, We eventually got into the classroom and made a beeline for the radiators to hang our wet blazers on. But there was no joy, or space, for that matter as the radiators were cram packed with caps, jackets and coats belonging to the boys who had gotten to school earlier. To make matters worse, the classroom was cold as ice, owing to the old heating system that was throughout the whole building. "*Imagine havin' tae dae an exam in here*" I said. "*Ah think the last time this place was warm wis during Queen Victoria's reign.*" "*For God's sake don't mention rain Alex, it reminds me how wet an' cauld ah am.*" replied Peter. "*Mark mah words, this place will be empty next week, we'll aw be aff wi' the bloody 'flu.*" The bell began ringing to start the morning session, just as the examiner, who happened to be Brother David, a member of the religious order of Marist Brothers, entered the room. "*Good morning all*" he began, then he uttered the words that I wasn't looking forward to "*Let's settle down and we shall begin.*" He then delegated some boys to distribute the exam papers and, upon getting the papers, a deathly hush descended, then all at once it was heads down and the exam had begun.

The morning seemed to drag by and, between my damp clothes and starting to feel the hunger pangs, by not having any breakfast, it was becoming an endurance test rather than a maths test. After, for what had been almost three hours of brain teasers, my eyes were getting heavy through lack of sleep, and any concentration I had was slowly ebbing away, but, like the proverbial boxer, I was saved by the bell, the lunch bell to be precise, and I can assure you it was music to my ears.

Usually in the good weather, we would miss out on the dinner hall and go outside the school for a walk, or go up to the canal which was at the top of High street and kick a ball around to pass the time.

I remember the time we once went over to the Necropolis to read the epitaphs on the tombstones. Now to get to the entrance of the cemetery we had to cross a bridge known as "*The Bridge of Sighs*" and directly underneath the bridge was Wishart Street and this, to me, was the quietest street in Glasgow. Any time of day I passed on my way to the Academy, this street was always deserted and there was an eerie stillness that seemed to linger there, the type of thing that makes you feel as though someone's watching you. There were four of us that day and we were taken aback by the sheer size of the place, but it was quite funny to read some of the inscriptions. One of the boys said "*Look at that one there, it read*: **Only Sleeping**: "*He's no half gonnae' get a shock when he wakes up*" he quipped. Then someone else said "*Aye, look at the date on it, 1836-1889 he's been sleepin' longer than Rip Van whatsit*. But the biggest surprise we got was seeing the monument of William Miller, the man who wrote the poem: Wee Willie Winkie. This is a poem that's been heard the world over by children which was sung to them by their mother:

Wee Willie Winkie rins through the toon,
Upstairs and downstairs in his night goon.
Knocking on the window and crying through the lock,
Are all the weans in their bed?
For its past ten o'clock.

Born in Glasgow, William Miller lived most of his life at No.4 Ark Lane in Dennistoun, and there is a commemorative plaque outside of the house where he was born, and can still be seen to this day.

I waited for Peter in the corridor and upon making our way to the dinner hall I asked him how he was getting on. He answered, in his usual satirical manner, "*Ah cannae get oan fer fallin' aff, ah think the only thing ah got right wis putting mah name at the top o' the paper and ahm no sure if ah spelt that right, worse still though who was sittin' right in behind me, was that wee sod Duff an' he's coughin' an' splutterin' aw ower the bloody place, mah jacket's wetter noo than it wis when ah came in this mornin'.*" "*Not to worry*" says I, "*When you get something hot to eat you'll be a new man, in fact you will feel like a young Greek God, ready at a mere whim to exert yourself to any challenge that comes your way. You shall face dangers that would put the shits up us ordinary mortals all for an extra bit of plum duff from the dinner lady who just happens to be chained to a pot of spotted dick."*

At that, I started to run to the dinner hall with Peter chasing after me shouting *"You'll hiv mair than a spotted dick if ah get a haud o' ye"* Once we got to the door, he said to me, *"All kidding aside Alex, if we get rice wi' oor dinner the day, they'll huv a mutiny oan their haunds because that will make it three times we've hud it this week, ahm beginning tae think there's a bloody paddy field at the back o' this school."* But, I could have strolled into a palace and not have been half content as I was at that moment the aroma of the hot food, coupled with the heat, was something to savour. Any meal given to me I would have devoured it, *"For hunger makes a good kitchen, and even if it had been only the dreaded rice, my plate would have been cleared of every morsel."* *"And, how did you find that meal Peter me lad?"* *"Can't complain, O wise sage from the mystic Gallowgate, only one thing amiss, ah don't feel like the Greek God, ah think am mair like wan o' thae greasy Greeks ye see comin' aff a boat doon at the Broomielaw."* *"Not so, young sir"* I countered *"You are a fine figure of a woman and the fates decree you shall go to the ball."* *"Talking of ball"* said Peter *"Ah don't see us gettin' a wee gemme o' fitba' the day, it's too wet."* *"What kind of talk is this I hear?"* I said," *Coming from a young salt of the sea, who single handedly sailed across Hogganfield Loch in an open rowing boat, without even a compass, or a jeely piece, have we seen the last of the great adventurers who would laugh in the face of danger, not to mention a bit of rain?"* *"Ah don't know aboot them, but you've seen the last o' me ah'm off tae the classroom tae get a bit o' heat."* *"That's mair like the Peter ah know."*

I said *"race ye up tae the radiators."* Most of the other lads had the same idea as us, because the class was nearly full when we got in, and Peter remarked *"So much for getting a heat at the radiators, if we died an' went tae hell we would never get near the fire, we would be stuck at the back an' aw these sods wid be at the front." "An whit did ye' think o' that Biology test? Ah don't see the reason fer gie'n us that, it's o.k. if ye' want tae work in hospitals, but ah think ah see enough casualties when ah look at some o' the punters comin' oot o' the boozers oan a weekend. "*

The second part of the exam began at one o'clock, but it wasn't as difficult as the morning session. Finding myself finishing the exam papers sooner than I had expected, I had a quick re-cap of the answers and, being quite satisfied that everything was all right, I sat and relaxed. Looking back, it had seemed a long week, the long studying at night and the lack of sleep, I realised how tired I really felt. Stifling a yawn and taking a glance at the clock, it showed half past three, not too bad only half an hour to go, so I gathered up my papers and made my way between the desks to the table where Brother David sat.

Like the majority of the teaching faculty, he was a fine tutor but unlike the others who could talk about football, or other sporting topics, he was a very quiet, phlegmatic man who would be found most times reading from books which he always had close at hand. The wonderful thing about him was, when he gave a lecture he could hold everyone's attention for hours on end, such was the gifted way this man had with words. He could spark dormant imaginations to life with a few sentences. Strangely though, he was also enigmatic because, for the life of me, I never understood how a man as clever as he was could be so unkempt and untidy. His clerical collar, once white, was yellowing with age, much akin to his cassock that seemed to be perpetually covered with chalk marks and all sorts of coloured stains. Upon hearing my approach to his table and, without even raising his head from the book he seemed engrossed in, he held out his hand, took my papers and dropped them onto the table that appeared to be as untidy as he was. There were boxes of chalk, blackboard dusters, pens, old jotters and a collection of all sorts of rubbish he had confiscated from pupils. The table resembled a battlefield of bric-a-brac and I'm of the impression that this was one of the table's tidier days. Making my way back to my own desk, I couldn't help thinking, "*Whatever happened to the cleanliness is next to Godliness bit that we were once taught?*"

As I sat at the desk, I began to watch the tiny rivulets of rain snaking their way down the windowpanes, at times appearing to be racing each other, then, as they got nearer the bottom, they would join together and create intricate patterns. After watching them for a short while, I began to think about my own personal race, which was to get to the tram stop as quickly as possible and then home. My thoughts were cut short as the bell for the end of class sounded, signalling a rushing stampede to get out the door and down the stairs as fast as you could.

Thinking back again to those days, it's still hard to envisage the mass of bodies that converged towards the main gate, only to be confronted by the P.E. teacher, whose duty for his sins, was to try and organise this mob into some semblance of orderly fashion. I believe he was assigned this task, owing to the fact that he was an ex-rugby player and had the countenance and scars to prove it. He stood around seven feet tall and, in passing him, if you were unfortunate enough to be shoved against this colossus; it resembled being hit by a rhino. He had a very peculiar habit though, because every now and then, he would select some poor unfortunate's head, slap it with the palm of his hand and say, "*That's for the MacGregors.*" To this day, I find myself smiling whenever it crosses my mind and I wonder what the reason was for this peculiarity.

I managed to get through the horde unscathed and out into the street, only to be met by a sleety wind that buffeted against my face with such a force, it felt as though I was being stung by a swarm of bees. My clothes were soaked through and as I squelched along, I must have looked a sorry sight and if, at that moment, I would have had the good fortune to meet the person who had stated these were going to be the best days of my life, I would have run them through with an umbrella (if I had one!).

At last, I got to the tram stop and my luck seemed to be in, a tram was just approaching the stop. A small queue had gathered there and as the tram stopped, the small group surged forward and then the cries went up. *"Ah'm afore you"* *"Hey stoap shovin'"* *"Mind that wee wummin there"* *"You wur at the back a meenit ago."* As I got nearer to the front, I noticed that it was a small man who was doing all the protesting, but, as he was making all the noise, he was getting edged backwards towards the back of the queue. The next thing I heard was the conductress dictating, and I mean that in every sense of the word, because she looked as though she could have given the P.E. teacher, a best of three falls contest and come out on top. *"O.K. three inside an' two upstairs."* By now it was every man for himself, it turned into a free for all, no quarter asked or given, elbows were used, knees and shoulders came into play and, all the while, a shout could be heard from the back *"Mind that wee wummin there."* It was the small man again doing his good deed for the day. By being quite small and also doing my own fair bit of pushing and wriggling, I found myself on the bottom deck of the tram, wedged between the passengers who were standing in the passageway.

The conductress, who had been up on the top deck, came back down and seeing how crowded it was bluntly ordered, *"Right, you two, aff, this caur's no movin' tae youse two get aff."* Her steely gaze was directed at the small man who had been doing all the shouting. *"Bit ah wis here first, ask that wee wummin' there."* The wee wummin' wasn't interested in his appeal, she had a seat and Sir Galahad could wait for the next bus as far as she was concerned. At last we got under way, along Duke St. passing the large prison that was used to incarcerate all types of prisoners. I remember my brother telling me that many years ago, around 12 executions were carried out in this jail, and the only woman (Susan Newell) ever to be executed in Scotland, met her death here. This was also the prison where John MacLean, the famous Socialist, was incarcerated and died at the age of 44. A shooting took place at the prison in 1921, it came about when the police had to escort a political prisoner from Ireland to the prison and some of his friends ambushed the police, causing one of the officers to be mortally wounded. This incident came to be known as *"The smashing of the van."* I know that some of my pals used to go to the outside wall of the prison to see the bullet holes that were supposed to be there, although I never came across anyone who had ever seen them. There was a little song that the young girls playing skipping ropes sang as they skipped.

> *"There is a happy land,*
> *doon Duke Street Jail,*
> *Where a' the prisoners stand,*
> *Washin' in a pail*
> *Ham an' eggs they never see,*
> *Dirty watter fur yer tea*
> *There they live in misery,*
> *Doon in Duke Street jail."*

Directly opposite the prison stood the Great Eastern Hotel, where the down and outs of the city were accommodated. I found it ironic that the unfortunate souls who lived in this run down hostel, did so under such a regally named abode. At the present time, there are ongoing plans to restore this wonderful old building into state-of-the-art flats.

My thoughts were brought back to the present, as I suddenly started feeling cold and damp, due to the rain on my saturated clothes seeping through to my skin, but I consoled myself with the thought that I would soon be at home sitting in front of an open fire, with a cup of warm tea in one hand and a comic in the other. The Bard knew what he was doing when he wrote, *"the best laid schemes"* because just as I was imagining the home comforts, a voice I knew rose above the chattering noise of the other passengers, it was that of Benny Feeney, a very good pal of mine, who actually lived a few doors from our house and, as luck would have it, went to the same school, but he was a year older than me, and a good few classes ahead in school terms.

Benny was a smashing bloke. He was the type that would go out of his way to help anyone who found themselves in need of a helping hand, nothing was ever too much bother for him and yet, if anyone had a strong reason to be grumpy and down in the mouth, it was him. He was born with a really bad squint in his eyes, and yet never complained or let this affliction get to him. Many a time I felt a bit sorry for him, as some of the other lads would make silly jibes calling him *"The one I love."* Which, to me, seemed in bad taste, but Benny being the type of guy he was, never took offence. The unusual thing was his name happened to be Paul Feeney, but there was an actor who used to appear in the Mack Sennett silent movies called Ben Turpin who also had a very bad squint, in fact it was worse than Paul's. So someone gave Paul the nick-name Ben, after the actor, and, needless to say, that name stuck . The one and only time I ever saw Benny take offence, was one night when one of the boys, who sometimes came to play football with us, brought a pal of his along for a game. After the game, we were all standing around having a laugh and telling jokes, when this idiot, who had been brought along, started having a few sarcastic remarks at Bennys squint, calling him *"Ivanhoe"* and such like. Now it so happened that this guy was wearing a pair of flaired trousers, which were the style at that time, so there and then, Benny saw his opportunity and made this comment that made this comedian look really foolish, He said to him *"There's only two types of people who wear that type of troosers—poofters an bullfighters, so huv ye' killed any bulls this week?"* It was one of the best stinging remarks I had heard in years, all the other boys were laughing so much at Benny's response that the stranger walked off with a petted lip and his tail between his legs and was never in our company again.

"Hey Alex, ah' saw ye' getting' oan at the last stoap, c'mon up, there's a few seats empty up here." What he failed to mention there was also a ticket inspector up there. I didn't want to go up for the main reason the people were allowed to smoke upstairs, so you felt as if you were in the middle of a thick fog, but knowing Benny was there, I ventured up. There were a few of the other lads there and the usual silly jokes and banter were being tossed around. I had just sat down when, all of a sudden, this wee officious, crabbit ticket inspector is standing there giving it the *"Any mair noise frae you lot an' yer aff"* speech. As we weren't causing any bother or upsetting anyone, a large man who was in the seat in front of me turned round and said in a loud voice, that even the inspector must surely have heard *"Don't bother yer heid wi' that yin boys, he's nothin' but a wee joabsworth, these cunts wid huv' loved tae be a polis' only they don't huv' the height, too short in the arse, know whit ah' mean?"* The boys all began to laugh as the inspector trudged off down the stairs and, to say he looked angry, was the understatement of the year. One of the lads sitting a bit further down from us called up *"Hey Alex, huv ye' got yer moothie' wi' ye?"* *"Aye, ah've got it in mah bag"* *"Good on ye' play somethin' then"* *"Whit will it be then?"* I asked. That was the last thing I should have done, because everybody seemed to have a song they wanted to hear *"Gie's Tennessee Ernie Ford's Sixteen* Ton*"* *"Naw, the Blue Tango"* it was getting out of hand, so I began to play a song that was really popular at the time, it was a song that Tommy Steele had in the charts called *"Singing the Blues"* and, as most people knew the tune, some joined in by either tapping their feet or whistling along. Next thing I knew, there was a hand on my shoulder and I got jerked to my feet. *"Right, Larry Adler, you were warned aboot the noise, you're aff."* It was the Glasgow Corporation's own wee keeper of the peace and goodwill and, by the time I realised what had happened, I was back to where I started twenty minutes previously, standing in the rain, along with my schoolbag and the inspector's favourite instrument, my moothie. After a bedraggled rain-sodden walk home, getting changed into dry clothes seemed to make things a shade brighter, although the same couldn't be said about out-of-doors.

The rain had stopped, but it had now developed back to the sleet which I had experienced earlier in the afternoon, only it now seemed colder and the only reason I know, is my mother asked me to go down to the wee shop at the corner of the street and get a pint of milk, otherwise wild horses couldn't have dragged me out into those elements. My sole intention was to hibernate at home all night, but as it only took a few minutes to get to the shop, I didn't really mind. I had just closed the front door behind me and was on my way to get the milk, when I heard the sound of someone running up the stairs. Suddenly, standing in front of me and gasping for breath as if he had finished the hundred yard dash, was Benny Feeney."*Whit's wrang wi' you?*" I asked him. "*Ye look as though ye're getting' chased by a ghost.*" "*Naw ah jist left the hoose tae come an' see ye', when ah wis caught in that snaw, efter puttin' oan dry claes tae, an that's me aw wet again. That's beside the point though, remember that guy that wis sittin' in front o' us oan the caur who wis tellin' us tae ignore yon Inspector guy? Well then, efter the Inspector turfed you aff the caur, he came back up the stairs an' that's when all hell broke loose, the man ah wis talkin' aboot said "Hey Adolph, ahm gonnae start singing, so get ready tae throw me aff." "Ah don't know whit the Inspector wis aboot tae say, but before he even opened his mooth tae say it, the guy landed wan right oan his chin an, decked him, ahm no kiddin, it wid huv put Joe Louis tae shame, whit a punch, the Inspector wis out tae the world, the best bit yet though had yet tae come because the fella just stepped o'er him an' as nonchalant as ye' please, sauntered doon the stairs an' aff the caur wi' the sound o' cheerin' an' whistlin' in his ears tae help him oan his wey.*" "Your hivvin' me on," I said "*Ah'm no'''*" Benny replied "*Ah'll tell ye something though, ye'll no find me oan any caurs oan Monday gaun tae school, auld gless jaw will be oan the look-out fer any o' the wans that wis oan that caur.*" "*Aye maybe yer right*" I said "*but we'll wait tae Monday tae see whit we're gonnae dae, anyway did you come oot in this weather jist tae tell me that?*" He stood there pondering, "*Oh aye ah' knew there wis somethin' else*" he said "*some o' the boys are goin' doon tae the café the night fer a wee while, d'ye fancy it? We could pass an hour or so, get's ye oot the hoose.*" I said alright and I would meet him later. After I had my supper, I went up to Benny's house, then later we left to meet Peter and two of our other pals, Mick Blair and Jim Tobin. We met Peter just as he was coming down the street and his first words to us were "*God in Govan it's no hauf freezin' the night, we need oor heids tested comin' oot oan a night like this, ah think we're in for mair snaw.*" "*Ah think yer spot on there*" said Benny. "*Have ye' no' seen Mick or Jim yet?*" Peter asked. "*Naw, were just goin' tae see if we can find them.*" "*Well we better get doon tae the Café, pronto, cos' ah think it'll be busy the night an' we want tae make sure we get a seat.*"

Just as we got to the door of the Café, it started to snow. "*Told ye so*" said Peter "*Ah should noo be known to all and sundry as the Oracle, as ah can see what the future hauds fer you lot.*" "*Mair like an orifice an' ah can see intae the future as well*" replied Benny. "*An ah can tell it's your turn tae dig intae yer' pocket an' get the Bovrils up.*" Going into the Café, we were greeted by Bob the owner "*Hullo there lads, how's things?*" "*Mah things are ready tae drap aff wi' the cauld*" replied Peter, "*there's a brass monkey oot there looking for a welder.*" "*So ye' think this is cauld, dae ye? Listen,*" said Bob, "*When ah wis in the army fightin' fer you lot, ah wis in Italy in January an' the snaw wis up tae oor knees an' ye didnae hear us moanin aboot the bloody cauld.*" On hearing this Peter started laughing "*Hey, listen tae General Montgomery here, bummin' he wis fightin' fer us, we've seen mair fightin at the street coarner when the pubs shut oan a Setterday night.*" Then, as if on cue, Benny chimed in "*Aye don't gies that patter, fightin' fer us, ye couldnae fight sleep.*" That got Bob started again, "*Tae think ah gave up three years of ma life fer ungrateful buggers like you lot, an all the thanks ah get is cheek.*" "*We didnae mean tae offend ye Bob, but be fair, at least ye goat a good de-mob suit fer yer troubles.*" Even Bob began to laugh at that quip from Benny. This sort of banter always made my night worthwhile. Just then Bob's wife Jean came through from the back of the shop, "*Whit's all the laughin' aboot? Oh ah might huv known, it's you lot, in tae annoy us again.*" "*Hi Jean, it's good tae see that happy, smiling, dour face of yours,*" I said "*It's nice to know we're wanted.*" Jean was a lovely person, well liked by everyone, she had a droll sense of humour and, when it came to a bit of banter, most times she won the war of words, hands down. "*By the way,*" said Bob, "*whit wid you lot like, or are ye jist in for a warm up?*" "*We'll gie' Jean the order if you don't mind, we don't want any mistakes.*" "*Christ, Jean, take the order quick, afore the last o' the big spenders leave, or we might end up in the poor hoose.*" "*Three bovrils, please Jean, and throw in a couple o' steel helmets, wi' the water biscuits yer man's away oan his war stories again, we'll aw be divin' fer cover when the bombs and bullets start flying aboot.*" Bob just shook his head and made for the back shop, chuckling as he went.

After having our hot drink and saying our goodnights to Bob and Jean, we made our way home. Just as we got to the corner of Bellfield Street, we met Mick Blair and Jim Tobin, "*Where did you two get tae? Ye were supposed tae meet us at Bobs café.*"

"*Ah know*" said Jim, "*Mah Maw wis late comin' back frae the shoaps wi mah auld man's supper, so that pit the hems oan me getting oot, ah hud tae watch the weans tae she came hame still we're here noo, whit's oan?*" "*Nothin' really*" said Benny, "*We're aw making oor way hame.* "*It's only hauf eight*" said Jim. "*A bit early fer bed. Listen, fancy a wee gemme o' cairds tae pass the rest o the night?*" "*Ah'm up fer that,*"said Benny, "*We might as well, seeing as there's nae school in the morning we can hae a long lie in bed.*"

It was nearly nine o'clock, therefore, we couldn't go to any of our houses at that late hour, so instead, we made our way to a place where we wouldn't be disturbed, or so we thought! Of all the places in the street we could have chosen, we just happened to choose the worst close in the whole of the Gallowgate. This place could have been mistaken for one of the prison cells on Devils Island. The stairs were covered with old pieces of paper that must have lain there for weeks on end and the paint, that was still clinging to the wall, was cracked and peeling, even the graffiti that must have been written, long before the war, was unreadable. Just as well, as I for one wasn't interested if Jean loved Dan or Kilroy had been there, someone was cooking cabbage and the stench was pungent, so we would have had to sit through this stink as we played cards. "*Haud oan, where dae we get a set o' cairds this time o' night?*" asked Benny. "*Nae worries*" said Jim "*Mah big brother's hame oan leave frae the Army and he's just been stationed at the Maryhill barracks, an ah saw him put a pack o' cairds in a drawer. Ah'll nip up tae the hoose an' get them.*"

After about twenty minutes, there was no sign of Jim. "*Where's he away tae fer thae cairds?*" asked Mick "*away tae the Maryhill Barracks? Either that or his faither's kept him in tae watch the weans again while he and his wife nip oot fer a swally.*" "*He better hurry up soon, or ah'm gonnae huv the boak wi' the reek aff that rotten cabbage, it smells as if somebody's bilin' up old working socks in a pot, this close must be the shit hole o' Glesca',*" At last, Jim showed up with the cards, telling us that they were at the back of the drawer and it took a while to find them, but, once we had a look at them Benny began to have a really loud bout of laughing. "*Ssshhhhh, you'll waken up everybody in the street*" said Mick. "*Nae wonder, wid ye' huv a look at them.*" answered Benny. "*Did the weans in the hoose use these tae cut their teeth oan?*" Benny was right, the cards were in a sorry state, they were all cracked and the corners were mostly bent upwards, plus the fact they were filthy "*Ah'm no touchin' them.*" I said. "*We'll aw catch some terrible disease, like scurvy or cardiology.* I don't know what that word meant, but it sounded good. "*Dae ye' want me tae take them back, ya shower o' ungrateful buggers?*" "*Aye and the first chance ye' get, toss them in the bloody fire, they're a health hazard.*" quipped Mick. "*Right, cut oot the nonsense and get the gemme started or we'll be here aw night.*" "*O.K., who's gonna be the dealer?*" "*Well seein' as they're ma cairds, ah think it should be me*" said Jim." "*Aw' right, jist get the gemme started.*"

"*Here we go. Get yer ante in the kitty, a penny in an' a penny a twist.*" We were all crouched down talking in whispers, so that no one could hear us, all that could be heard was the soft putt, putting of the old gas mantle of the stairway light, which gave off an eerie, yellowish glow, causing us to have a jaundiced palour. The only other noise was the clinking of the coppers as they were put into the kitty. Talking of coppers, as we were so engrossed in the game, no one heard the noise of someone climbing the stairs. I was sitting facing Mick and I could see his eyes widening and his mouth slowly opening as though he wanted to say something but couldn't find the words. Suddenly, we all heard this booming voice, *"Whit huv we got here then, a gambling school?"* It was the local beat policeman, Matt Fleming.

The reason I knew his name was because, like my Father, Matt was a pigeon fancier and he also bred them as a hobby. My father would often take me along with him when he was buying some of the pigeons from Matt and it was amazing to see the small birds that had just emerged from their eggs. I remember that once I held one of the small birds and it was a strange feeling to look down on this tiny creature as it nestled in the warmth of my hands, that was the reason that I knew who Matt was, my misfortune was, he also remembered me. *"Right, who do we have here then?"* He began to rhyme us all off *"Feeney, Tobin, Taylor, Donnelly and Blair, does your mither an' faither huv any idea whit your up tae?"* He then proceeded to line us all up against the wall, we all stood looking at the ground as big Matt lectured us about how playing for money could somehow lead us into a life of all sorts of things, then came the clincher *"Now, whit dae ye want, a kick on the arse or put in jail?*

I can still see it and feel it now, we all bent over and got a size fourteen where the sun didn't shine and, be rest-assured, this guy didn't miss. I can still hear the sound of his boot making contact, talk about the long arm of the law, this was certainly the long legged boot of the law. I don't believe any of us sat down for the rest of that week. *"Off ye' go now and don't let me find any of you bad lads up tae yer tricks again, or it will be the jail fer ye' next time!"* But, before he let us go home, he took the few halfpennies that we were playing for and put them in his pocket. If I thought that was bad, worse was to come, for a few days later my Mother got me aside and told me how big Matt had a word with her about me getting caught playing cards. So, not only did I get a sore backside, I also got a clip on my ear for my troubles.

A few days later I met Mick again and his first words were "*Whit dae ye' think o' that big sod taking oor money and stashin' it in his pocket? Ye cannie trust naebody these days.*" Another occurrence gave us cause to remember big Matt shortly after our gambling escapade. At the rear of one of the tenements, there happened to be a large piece of land across from the building where we lived and, on a Sunday, the pigeon fanciers would gather there to talk about their pigeons and whose bird was breeding, or racing in the coming week. Another reason they all met there was because one of the men had a pigeon loft on top of one of the roofs, so they could stand and watch the coming and goings of the birds. The men would all stand with their backs against the wall, craning their necks, looking skywards, to watch the birds homing in on the loft. I can still visualize these men, they all appeared to be dressed the same, with their caps low over their eyes and silk scarves tucked into their waistcoats, this seemed to be the dress code of the pigeon brigade.

This particular Sunday morning there happened to be a pitch and toss school in progress. This was a game where a man would get two pennies, balance them on two fingers of his hand and throw them up in the air, the object of the game was to try and get the two coins to land on the ground with both faces up. The others watching would bet for or against the coins landing that way, so they would put their money on the ground to show if they were for or against how the coins would land. While all this was going on, most of the boys were playing football, suddenly two policemen and a few plain clothes detectives arrived on the scene, they had all come into the backcourt through separate closes, surrounding everyone who happened to be there and also closing off any chance of anyone getting away. The moment the police were spotted, all the gamblers ran and stood beside the men who were watching the pigeons and mingled with them, so the police couldn't tell who was who. This ploy worked for the gamblers, but it also worked out well for the boys that were playing with the ball. None of the gamblers were getting their collars felt that time, but, as the police were looking at all the men standing there, big Matt, who fortunately for us, was one of the policemen, sauntered over to where all the money belonging to the men who had been gambling, was lying and asked "*Who belongs to this money*? As no one declared it was theirs, big Matt picked it all up and then called over Jim Tobin, "*Here son, ah found this money, so seein' it disnae belang tae anybody, ye' can go and buy some lemonade fer you and your pals.*"

The gamblers faces were all grimacing and you could sense their anger, they must have been seething to see their money going to buy sweeties and lemonade, but we were off before the polis' left and they had any chance of getting it back and that made big Matt a hero in our eyes. But, months later, I was telling Jean, the café owner, about what happened that day and also about the night big Matt took our money and put it in his pocket and kept it, but Jean made me realise there was more to big Matt than we thought. She told me that he had come into her shop for a chat and then put the money that he took from us into a small charity bag that was meant for the war blind soldiers at Erskine Hospital. Yes, big Matt was a real hero who went unnoticed, not only was he a big man in our eyes, but he was also big in stature. There may have been genuine members of the police force, but, as far as I was concerned, they were few and far between.

Too many of Glasgow's finest seemed to be a law unto themselves and used their uniform to take liberties and exert their authority on the public for their own sadistic pleasure. Two of the most notorious of them, were a couple of rascals who were known to most of the Gallowgate fraternity as John the B. and Ginger. Whenever you saw these guys coming towards you, it was always a good idea to make yourself scarce, otherwise, they would have you standing explaining where you had been, where were you going, asking all sorts of personal questions in a way that always seemed to be threatening, add to that, they were sadistic to the point where they thought nothing of punching men who were perhaps too drunk in their eyes, before hauling them down to the local police station in Tobago Street.

As much as big Matt was liked, these men were hated. I remember the Saturday night four of my pals and I had just come from the Orient cinema, it was around half past eight when we got to our street and, as we usually did, we stood talking for a while before going our separate ways. I was just about to leave when I heard the voice, "*Just stay where you are.*" It was The B and another constable. He took all our names and the following Saturday, a court summons came through the post, letting me and all the others know that we were to appear at the Sheriff court on the charge of loitering. All my pals and I appeared and were all fined 10 shillings. What really angered me was the injustice of it all, knowing that we had all been innocent, and yet my Mother had to pay this fine, even though she was just about making ends meet.

This was one of the many episodes that made many folk have no respect for the police, although one of the older boys, Gino Valerio, had his own warped scheme for getting his revenge on the beat polis'. Back in the earlier days, all the stores had large padlocks on their shop doors, so when the polis' on the beat passed along the shop fronts, he would tug on the lock making sure it was properly locked. So what Gino would do was get a stick and put some dogs excrement on the end of it and then smear the padlock and, more often than not, the polis' would get a handful of dog shit, which wasn't too pleasant, to say the least. I must admit though, all the boys thought it was hilarious. This went on for weeks, but as the man said "*All good things must come to an end*" as Gino was about to find out.

He was making his way home one night, when he was pulled into one of the street doorways by two big, sturdy polis'. One held Gino's hand out and the other smashed it with a truncheon, breaking three of Gino's fingers and fracturing his wrist. The word was out that someone had tipped off the polis' who the culprit was and I believe, if that person had ever been found out, he would have been wise to leave the country for the good of his own health, as he would have had more than a few broken fingers to worry about.

Things had gone really quiet for a while. In fact, it was starting to get to the boring stage when out of the blue we had something to look forward to. One afternoon some of the usual cronies were standing at the street corner, when who should come along but Jim Tobin. *"Where have you been hiding the past few days?"* asked Benny. *"Och, ah got a job wi' Gemmel's Dairies deliverin' milk. The only thing is it's a five o'clock start in the mornin' but it gets me a few pounds at the weekend, an' the tips are good. The only thing is, ah finish aboot hauf eight and then it's intae school and, by the end of the day, ahm shagged oot."* *"We thought ye had emigrated"* said Feeney. *"Naw, listen stupid arse, aw kiddin' aside, ah wis daen ma round this mornin' an who should ah see but Jackie Ross, ye know him frae Cubie Street? Well it turns oot he's a bit o' a boxer, an he wis oot runnin' this mornin'. He's got a fight on in a few weeks an this is him oot trainin'. His faither says that he's got a manager an' this guy thinks Jackie can go a long way in this boxin' gemme."* Peter said, *"Ah wonder if that's the same fella ah' know that wis in the Shell Harriers and wis supposed tae be a long distance runner. If it is the same guy, the Harriers got rid o' him. It turned oot the only thing that wis good at runnin' wis his nose."* *"Trust you tae say that."* said Jim. *"He had all the boxin' gear oan, shoart troosers, heavy sweater, towel roon the neck, the lot, an forbye, who's gonnae go oot runnin' an sweatin' at that time in the mornin'?"* asked Jim." *"Maybe he's oot deliverin' milk."* laughed Peter.

That started us all off, we were helpless with laughter at that remark. *"Sod aff you lot, ah'm away up tae the hoose fer some tea, ah'll see you'se aw later."* With that, Jim was off home.

Seemingly, Jackie Ross's father was in the local pubs telling anyone who would listen how his son was going to be a boxer and that his manager had great faith in him to become really good at the boxing, but, as he was just beginning, he had to start at the lower ranks of his new profession and that was going to be the boxing booths at Glasgow Green carnival.

I remember asking my brother if the boxers at these booths were any good, and he told me that it was all the old ex-boxers who now fought there, eeking out a living for themselves, by going in the ring and fighting men who thought they could last for three rounds. If anyone beat them, they got five pounds for going the distance with these old fighters, who were all well past their glory days. But, very few of the challengers managed to get the better of them. So when the time came for Jackie's first fight, which was going to be the Saturday afternoon, all the boys trooped down to the Glasgow Green, where Jackie was about to make his debut, which, to all intents and purposes, was pointing our local hero to new horizons.

The carnival always came to the Glasgow Green from early June until the end of August. During these months, the Glasgow Fair fortnight began, that's when all the factories would close down to let the workers have a two-week break and a chance for them to have a holiday, which was usually a trip down to the coast for Maw, Paw and the weans where they could all spend a few days together at the seaside.

When we arrived at the carnival, it was the same as any other year, the smell of greasy hamburgers, chips and onions wafting up your nostrils, then there was the cacophony of loud music, the screaming of girls on the roundabouts and the dodgem cars, the barkers shouting you over to try and win a prize at the different stalls and the ear splitting sounds of the large engines that made the machines go spinning round at terrific speeds. The carnival never ever appealed to me and this was one of the reasons, too much noise and the fact that the air always had a heavy stench of petrol and diesel fumes, also the dust that was kicked up by the heavy traffic by the public walking around always gave me a stuffy, sickly feeling in my throat. If ever you wanted a headache, this was the place to go, but I knew that as soon as I had seen the fight, I would be leaving for home.

We eventually got to the booth where the bouts took place. It was a large marquis with a small platform at the door, above which hung pictures of boxers, for example, Benny Lynch. I knew of this particular boxer from the photos I had seen, and the stories I had heard of him, but I hadn't a clue about the rest. There were large crowds all milling about and it appeared that the whole of the district had turned up to see this fight. After a short while, the MC came onto the stage with a large megaphone and gave a short talk about how some great fighters had started their careers at this very booth and how he was looking forward to seeing some of the young men who had the skill to make his name in the noble art in future years. Then, as if on cue, three boxers came out from behind an old piece of canvas, which was a makeshift door, and climbed onto the stage. They then began to do a bit of shadow boxing, moving around, ducking and weaving, the sort of thing that you sometimes saw in the boxing movies, although they didn't look anything like great boxers to me. But how would I know, I wasn't a fan of boxing.

The MC then asked if there was anyone in the crowd who would like to try their skill against any of his fighters and, all at once, a big cheer went up when Jackie raised his hand. He was then taken into the tent to get prepared for the fight. As we all stood waiting, no one else volunteered, so we all paid our entrance money and went through the small door into the booth. The first thing that caught your eye was an old dilapidated boxing ring, where the floor seemed to be just above eye level, perhaps that was to stop you from seeing the old blood stains on the canvas, but it that didn't prevent you, then the dust that arose from the canvas, whenever anyone walked across the ring, would. We all had to stand about until the place was filled to capacity, but, what helped to pass the time was watching a man walking around the booth chasing young boys who were trying to gain entrance by sneaking in under the bottom of the tent. As he would chase one boy, another head would come up from another part of the canvas. Some of the crowd were pointing to parts where no one was trying to get in, just to watch him running all over the place.

Suddenly, the place went quiet, as into the ring stepped the man with a megaphone in his hand and his booming voice stated that the boxing was about to begin. He began by saying that, due to the lack of a response from any others who wanted to try their skill against any of his fighters, there would be only one bout and that was to be between a local lad, young Jackie Ross, and his man who went by the name of "Spider Kelly." As the MC was getting prepared to get the show underway, Jackie was giving us the boxing gloves above the head and a wee foot shuffle routine, holding on to the ropes and bending at the knees, he really looked the part, then into the ring came Spider. *"Fer God's sake"* said Peter, *"he looks like a bloody ape, wid ye' look at the length o' his airms, he'll murder the poor sod."* Spider's head looked as if it had been hit by a moving bus and I wouldn't have been surprised to know that the bus came off worse. His nose was flat as a witch's tit and I'm positive he was cross-eyed, this guy would have scared a ghost. I don't know how Jackie was feeling but, we were positive we would need to be ready to summon an ambulance.

The first bell sounded and the bout got underway, Jackie came out quite cautiously, throwing a left jab here and there, sometimes getting in on the target but not doing too much damage. Then the advice from the crowd started to ring out *"Stoap dancin' hit the bugger, c'mon Jackie, stiffen that old cunt, gie him a dull wan son."* Not a lot seemed to be happening, but Jackie was giving a good account of himself. While Spider was taking a few soft punches, there was a lot of moving about, but not a lot of action, but that was about to change. The bell rang, the first round was over. Jackie's dad was at his corner turning round and giving everyone the thumbs up sign. I began to have a bit of faith now, the boy was doing well. The bell sounded again for the second round, but, owing to the noise and shouts from the crowd, Jackie seemed not to hear it. That didn't stop Spider, because he was off his seat and across he ring before poor Jackie realised what was happening. Spider's hand was a blur as three left stinging jabs connected with Jackie's head and they were so fast he appeared to be nodding in agreement as his head went back and forth. It was just as we feared, Spider had Jackie all over the ring. I don't think he knew where the next punch was coming from, then MAYHEM! I think Jackie believed that Spider had taken an unfair advantage of him, so in an uncontrollable rage, ran over threw his arms round Spider, head butted him and then kicked him in the groin and, within minutes, all the other boxing friends of Spider were in the ring, punches were being thrown at anything that moved, in fact, people were stepping over the referee, who was lying prostrate on the floor. There seemed to be more bodies in the ring than what there was out of it. Eventually, the polis' came and a bit of order was restored, and the last thing I remember hearing was MC going on about how Jackie had brought the name of the noble boxing profession into disrepute with his disgraceful behaviour.

As we were all making our way home, Peter uttered a statement which was going through all of our minds *"That cunt Jackie should huv stayed being a runner, it wid huv been handy fer him tae get away frae the Spider's punches. Aye and it wid huv saved us a coupla' boab, we wid huv been better tryin' tae win a cokeynut."* said Jim. Who said sportsmanship was dead? Peter then had us all doubled up laughing when he said *"Just imagine, Spider can get a wee farm an´ take up farming now."* *"Whit makes ye' think that?* I asked. *"Well, when Jackie hit him a kick on the balls, he gave him a coupla´ achers."*

Not long after his one and only fight, we heard that Jackie had moved down south to Manchester to get a job. I think the only boxing he'll do down there is if he becomes an undertaker.

That night we all went to the cinema, the Orient picture hall, to be precise, to see the movie: **The Charge Of The Light**

Brigade. It was the usual old story, Errol Flynn and his pals winning the battle, then at the very end, Errol getting the good looking dame, in fact, we nearly all got thrown out, all because we began singing a parody we all knew, it was sung to the tune of **The Garry Owen**, it went something like:

> *Errol Flynn got thirty days*
> *For lookin' up a wummin's claes*
> *An all he seen was sixty flaes*
> *Chargin' intae battle*

Then just before the cartoons started, the cinema attendant walked down the aisles, carrying this big brass contraption that looked every bit like a large bicycle pump, and started spraying this fine mist of DDT upwards towards the ceiling. This stuff was moist and mingled with the heavy clouds of cigarette smoke that hung in the air, it was also meant to kill germs and freshen the air, but all it did was to come within a fraction of suffocating the people sitting in the aisle seats, as it drifted down on top of them. After a short time, there was a continuous outbreak of coughing and sneezing, as the fine film of disinfectant, which was now mixed with the smoke, was inhaled. Everyone, who was watching the movie, was being distracted by the affected coughers standing up and stumbling in the dark, as they tried to find another seat to get clear of the DDT drizzle, as it filtered downwards. Then the shouts could be heard "*Sit doon a cannae see through ye.*'" "*Hurry up an'*"*move yersel' big heid.*" Then, to make matters worse, someone began to light up a **Pasha** cigarette and the smell from these cancer sticks, as they were commonly known, was like inhaling horses manure and people swore that's what they were made from. These cigarettes were sold during the war and, as all other types of tobacco were scarce, this was the last resort for the smokers and they must have been really desperate if they bought these things to smoke.

Trying to watch the film was becoming farcical, because some of the crowd in the balcony began to drop all sorts of objects onto the people below, bits of orange peel, ice cream cartons and paper straws, etc. This continued until the attendants went up, got the culprits and threw them out. Then, just as we all began to settle down, the picture broke up and froze for a few minutes. That was the signal for an outbreak of booing and feet stomping. It sounded like a herd of cattle rampaging through the cinema, this didn't cease until the picture was restored and was up and running again. Actually, we had a better laugh at this carry on, than watching the movie. Suddenly, all hell broke loose, a voice further down towards the screen gave out a cry, "*San Toi*" within a minute there were about twenty guys all standing up throwing punches, swinging all sorts of weapons and whatever came to hand, the **Toi** was a local gang who had spotted members of another gang at the same film. That was the signal for all the audience to make a beeline for the exits, as they didn't want to be caught up in the gang fight. This was a regular occurence in these small local cinemas, so it came as no surprise. Strangely enough, it didn't deter people from going out to the movies, mainly because it was a cheap night out and you didn't have to travel too far to see a film.

My outstanding memory of the Orient cinema was the small van that always sat outside, selling hot rolls. As you came out, you could buy them, all freshly baked, straight from the oven. The smell, taste and texture of the rolls were delicious. I always bought about a half dozen, then I would make my way home fast as my legs would carry me, trying my best to keep them warm before I got home. On a cold winter night, as the rest of the family were asleep in bed, it was so relaxing to sit alone in the darkness in front of the open coal fire, cocooned in the warmth, as the flames threw up, moving, life-like shadows on the walls. Eating hot buttered rolls and sipping a cup of tea, next to the welcoming fire, to me was one of the creature comforts of life. The other luxury afforded me, was going to bed, crawling under the blankets and reading a few chapters of a book, with the light from a small bedside lamp, which gave off a soft glow, there was a wonderful feeling of cosiness and contentment, then laying down the book, turning off the light, pulling the bedclothes up to my shoulders, resting my head on my pillow, I would be asleep within minutes.

The next morning I was going down to Saint Mary's chapel in Abercrombie Street to meet Ed McMenemy, a boy that I had gone to school with. I had met him the previous week and he told me that most of the Saint Mary's boys' guild team gathered at the old graveyard behind the chapel to play football. I let Peter and Benny know about the football, but they weren't interested. So off I went to meet up with Ed, who introduced me to some of the boys before going into Mass. The boys, who were mainly Catholic, would go to Mass, then come out and then get two teams, picked at random, then get the game started. Then it was hell for leather, no quarter given, I thought they were playing for World Cup medals the way they went about their business. I'd played in hard games before, but this was like a war.

What I found strange was the fact that we were running over old gravestones that were lying flat and some of the epitaphs could still be read, but most of them were covered in moss and lichens. I often wonder if there are still some young people playing there, if so, I hope their games are a bit tamer. As our game wore on, some of the older men took part, it now seemed to be around fourteen on each side, you were lucky to get a glimpse of the ball, far less a kick. There was one chap there called Max and, whenever he got the ball, he seemed to get the ball stuck between his feet, then stumble and fall. At first I thought he was being pushed around by the taller, heavier men, but I was told this happened to him every time he played, One of the men said to him, "*Max if ye' played fitba' wi' yer arse, you wid get a gemme fer Scotland.*" After the game ended, we all sat down for a breather with our backs against the wall and listened to the older lads as they filled our heads with stories about what they got up to during the week, and the girls that they had taken home from the dancing. Talk about the tall story club, I think most of them were founding members.

We were getting outrageous tales about beautiful women from guys with faces that would frighten weans. What made me laugh was that some of the boys were sitting there with their mouths gaping open, listening to this garbage.

The good thing that came out from that day was the fact that I met two men who gave me a new outlook on life. One was Father Tony Beckett, and the other a man called John Rice. John was watching us playing that day and afterwards came over to speak to some of the boys who played for the boy's guild team. John was a grown man and was a good deal older than the rest of us. He worked as a school janitor, but he somehow always found the time to keep the boys interested in all types of sport, especially football, badminton and physical fitness. John was the main reason that I became a member of the boy's guild.

He began speaking to me after the football and said he hadn't seen me with the rest of the boys before and asked, if interested, I could come down and train with the guild. Having been told by Ed that the guild had a good football team and the great times they had playing five-a-side games and then following up with a game of badminton, a game that I always had wanted to learn, was music to my ears. I didn't have to be asked twice. I arranged to meet Ed on the following Tuesday and that's when I joined the boy's guild. These were some of the greatest years of my life, mingling with new friends and getting to play football most Saturdays, Then going to the dancing in St. Mary's church hall.

Later on in life, as I grew older, I began to realise that John Rice got a great deal of enjoyment from watching all the boys develop into young men. These were the boys who would, more than likely, have been hanging around street corners, with nothing to do and nowhere to go. He gave us all something to look forward to and somewhere to go on certain nights. He also instilled in us that it wasn't all about winning. The aim was to take part and enjoy any game you took part in. John was the man who was instrumental in taking the well known and admired footballer, Tommy Burns, who also played for Saint Mary's guild, to Celtic Park. This was where Tommy became an instant favourite of the fans and spent a wonderful career with Celtic and eventually went on to play for Scotland.

Prior to me leaving the guild, John began organizing holidays for the boys who were members of the guild. They would go to Spain and other destinations, where they all had wonderful times. To this day, I don't think John received the accolades he deserved for the efforts that he contributed in keeping all the boys together as a group. Then, when we outgrew the guild, other young boys took our place and John was still there to bring out the camaraderie and his know-how to the new batch of boys.

Father Beckett was a young priest, who had just arrived at the parish and had yet to meet some of the parishioners. He soon got to know most of the boys, as we were down at football training with John, every Tuesday and Thursday. Father Tony, as he soon became known, was very popular, especially with all the younger folk, he developed a great rapport with everyone who came to know him.

He had an aura of gentleness about him and was the first priest that I had ever seen, outside the chapel, minus his dog collar. To me, this was wonderful, it seemed to cast off the cloak of forced reverence that was often shown to men of the cloth, even if you didn't respect their outlook or their beliefs i.e. "*Don't question or contradict anything they might say, accept what they believe with blind faith.*" Father Tony wasn't that type of priest, he would sit as long as you wanted, debating all sorts of subjects, listening and then giving his slant on things. He was a breath of fresh air and it was a pleasure to be in his company. One example of how he could connect with people shone through, for instance, as I remember one night after the boys had finished training, he invited us all into the chapel house, where he asked the housekeeper make enough tea and toast for all of us. Then he put on a record and asked us what we thought of the most recent singer in the charts. I, for one, was blown away as I heard for the first time the voice of Johnnie Mathis, who sang a song called **A Certain Smile** and we all agreed that this new "kid on the block" was going to be a huge star. At least, we all proved we were first class critics, as everyone now knows, Mathis is now a world-wide entertainer.

I've met and known many a priest in my lifetime, but there will always be a special place in my thoughts for Father Anthony Beckett. On the subject of priests, John Rice arranged a game of football between a team of priests and the boys who played for the guild. It was to be played over at the Glasgow Green football pitches, and, if we thought we were in for a quiet kick about, we were sadly mistaken. These guys were no shrinking violets, they were kicking everything above ground except the ball, their motto seemed to be "*Never mind the ba' get oan wi' the gemme*" they were assailants. The final whistle to end the game couldn't come soon enough for me, the reason being, once you've been kicked up into the air a dozen times, by a giant of a man, you begin to lose interest.

After the game ended, I didn't shake hands with this priest, not because I was a poor sport, but the truth was, I didn't want my fingers crushed. As we all trooped off the park, one of the boys said "*They didnae half gie us a doin', maybe they thought we were a' protestants.*" Then one of the other boys said to me "*That priest you were playin' against, should huv a leash oan that dog collar o' his, he wis a big, bloody animal, yer lucky he didnae bite yer legs, never mind kickin' them.*"

Then it started, "*Ur ye' sure John Rice said priests, wis it no' beasts?*"

The priests all got their characters that afternoon, as we all made our way back home.

It was almost six o'clock. I was feeling a bit tired and leg weary, so I decided to get the 46 bus, which went to the Cranhill housing scheme, and also stopped at the Gallowgate which meant that I had only a short distance walk to get home. After a few minutes, the bus came along and, as I stepped on, I noticed that sitting on the very first seat was a man holding a long wooden pole, which to me looked like a broom handle.

As he stood up and made for the door, I sat on the seat that he had been sitting on. It so happened this wasn't one of the newer type of buses and didn't have automatic doors that opened and closed as the bus stopped. The door of this bus was open all the time and had an upright steel bar at the door, so that the passengers could hold onto as they were getting ready to alight onto the street.

I sat on the seat that he had been sitting on and watched as he stood at the door, holding onto the steel bar with one hand and holding the wooden broom handle in his other. The bus had to slow down on the main road, as it had to make a right turn into Abercromby Street. Now there happened to be a public house right on the corner and, as the bus began to pick up speed, a man came out of the pub, saw the bus as it was passing by and he made a beeline for the platform. This was where the chap with the broom handle was standing, waiting to get off at the next stop, but as he leapt onto the platform, instead of grabbing hold of the steel bar, he caught hold of the broom handle, fell backwards, taking with him the poor guy who was standing there minding his own business. I couldn't believe my eyes at what was taking place and the last thing that I saw, was the two of them rolling about the street punching lumps out of each other. I must admit, I had a good laugh at this scenario that had just taken place, and the first thing that crossed my mind was that this could have made a great scene for a Charlie Chaplin movie.

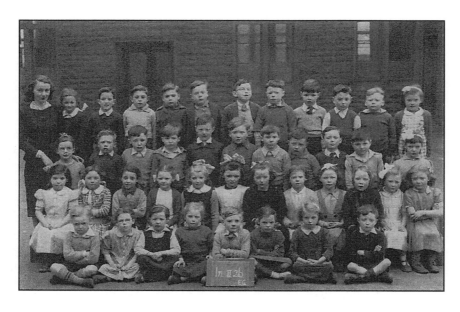

**Alex school photo circa 1947—top row,
fourth child from the left**

The Parade Picture House

**St.Mungo's Academy,
Parson Street, Townhead**

**The Orient Picture House,
Gallowgate, Glasgow**

1999
SAINT ANNE'S SCHOOL

"Just follow me" the young janitor instructed, *"the meters are in the boiler room, I suppose you've no' been here before? Ah'll show ye' where they are."* If only he knew that I had stood here long before he had ever heard of Saint Anne's primary school, some fifty odd years previously, to be exact. But, this was the first time I had returned since leaving here at the age of eleven to go to Saint Mungo's Academy, which happened to be the secondary school I attended after the eleven plus exam. I attended St. Mungo's until I was fifteen, and I often looked back with wonderful reflections to the happy times that I had spent at the Academy,

I always had a soft spot for Saint Anne's. It was a very small primary school, situated in David Street just off the Gallowgate. I had never imagined I would ever be back again and the only reason I found myself standing in the place, that held so many fond memories for me, was that I was employed by the Scottish Power Electricity Company and was sent to inspect the meters. Afterwards, as I was making my way out of the building, I happened to glance into one of the classrooms and it all came flooding back, wonderful memories of another time. The smells that always seemed to linger as you entered the classroom, the strong aroma of disinfectant that was used by the cleaning ladies to scrub the wooden floors and the polish that they put on the desks.

I found myself in a time warp that took me all the way back to the very first day that I set foot in Saint Anne's school. "*Where did the time go? I* asked myself. This is the puzzling question that enters the head of most people as we grow older as we try to capture the halcyon days of those bygone years. All the ifs, ands and buts rise to the surface, as we recall the decisions that we made as the future beckoned us towards our destiny. I can recall my first day at school as if it were yesterday. I was told for weeks previously that I would be starting school and it would be so much fun, I would be meeting lots of new friends that I could play games with and a teacher there who was going to teach me how to read stories and she would give me paper and crayons to draw with. This all sounded like a dream come true and I couldn't wait to start, but came the day when I actually had to go to this wonderful place, I started to have second thoughts.

To begin with, I never been up and out of bed at this time in the morning and it was a bit unusual to find myself getting washed and dressed at this early hour. After having my face washed at the old brass swan necked water tap and putting on the new clothes that had been bought for me, my sister began fussing about me, making sure my hair was tidy and everything else was in place, she looked more excited than I did and that is when I began to feel frightened. Even at that young age, I seemed to realize that I would be away from the rest of the family, especially my younger sister Anne, as we were really close, and would play together for hours on end. Thinking about this, I began to get upset and kept saying to my mother that I didn't want to go. I remember my sister Lizzie telling me that only babies stayed at home with their mother and I had to be a big boy to attend school. She also promised to buy me sweeties and a comic if I went to school. The small bribe did the trick. This was music to my ears, as it wasn't everyday you got a treat like this.

So with Lizzie holding my hand, off we went. I can't remember much about getting there, but I do recall seeing this large grey building with what seemed to have hundreds of windows, spiked railings all around the walls and two huge iron gates. As my sister took me through the iron gates, that's when I began to get really scared, although little did I know that the worst was yet to come. Everywhere I looked there were boys and girls everywhere, all being taken by the hand and all walking in the same direction as we were. I could see that some were crying and others digging in their heels and having to be half dragged along towards a door where stood an old silver-headed lady. She was, as I recall, quite small and dressed from head to toe in black, she had very pale, wrinkled skin and wore a pair of spectacles that appeared to be perched on the very tip of her nose. She had pieces of paper in her hands and on passing her, your guardian gave your name which was then duly crossed off. All the boys and girls were then taken into this room, which was going to be our very first classroom on the long journey of many other classrooms, where we would be taught our three Rs until we were older, but not always, as it turned out to be, wiser.

When it was time for the people, who brought us here, to leave, they seemed to be trying to get out the door without being noticed. One or two managed to get out, but when we realized we were going to be left alone with this strange woman, all hell broke loose, one girl began to cry and everyone else followed suit. Some were trying to get out the door, some were screaming their heads off, and that was just the boys! The girls seemed to become hysterical, it was utter bedlam and the poor teacher had to try and establish some control over this mayhem. Eventually, a bit of order was restored, one of the reasons being, Miss Heefie brought our attention to a large, black, wooden rocking horse that stood in the corner of the room and told us that, if we were nice and quiet, the big horse would let us sit on him. Within no time at all, the noise died away and we all stood in line for our turn to get onto the horse. Everything was going great as the teacher put one pupil after another onto the saddle and pushed the horse so that it moved back and forth, As luck would have it, I was behind a girl who was still really upset but she still got lifted onto the horse and got rocked back and forth until she settled down and stopped crying. As she got taken down, I was lifted on and, after a few minutes, felt the seat of my trousers damp, the saddle was like a wet sponge. The reason being, the girl who was on the horse before me, had soiled her pants and the teacher hadn't noticed it when she lifted her down. So, as the saddle had to be washed, the rest of the class didn't get their turn on the rocking horse, but they were the lucky ones, as I had to sit on a cold, wooden desk seat with my wet trousers for the rest of the morning until it was time to go home.

After school, I was met by my sister and, true to her word, I got my sweeties but, if I thought this was going to be a regular treat, I had another think coming, it never happened again! After a few days, I began to get to know most of my classmates and as usually happens began to forge a friendship with a certain few, two of whom spring to mind. For instance, they were James Nixon and John Downie. Nixon had a wonderful ear for music and, even for a boy so young, he could play the accordion and harmonica, it was more commonly known as a *moothie,* so well. After hearing him play, some of the other pupils, myself being one, got the music bug and began to try and copy him. Funnily enough, he taught me to play the mouth organ, much to my chagrin, as you will have ready earlier in this story.

Another thing that sticks in my mind, was the school nurse who showed up once a fortnight. She would look at the inside of your ears and then proceed to pull this very fine toothed comb through your hair to see if you had a clean head, that meant finding no nits, as they were the eggs of a louse. I can still feel the pain of this comb as she slowly dragged it through my hair and, while she was doing this, she was also taking large clumps of hair from your scalp. After she had seen the entire class, the place looked like a barber's shop floor—how most of the pupils weren't bald by the time they left that school, I'll never know.

Lots of the pupils had these nits through no fault of their own, but it amazes me that we all didn't have this affliction, as the main reason for getting them was by not having your hair washed regularly. But, to be truthful, we were fortunate to be having a bath twice a week, so it was no mean feat to escape them. I still remember my mother telling me to stay away from anyone who had a dirty head, but what was I supposed to do? When everybody was in the playground and you wanted to take part in the games they were playing, did you ask them if they had a dirty head?

Walking past the other classrooms brought their own memories, for instance the time that Mr. Gillespie had to speak to a girl, Isabella Rae (who was breaking her heart crying) and explain to her that there was no Santa Claus. Poor wee soul, that rascal Nixon had let the cat out of the bag, she was only nine years of age too!

We then passed onto a class, where I learned more in the space of a year than I had in the five years previously. This was where Miss Anna Melone taught. She was a small lady who, when it came to getting the best out of her young charges, was peerless. Nothing was ever too much trouble for her. She would take all the time that was needed to make sure that you understood the problem. She was always there for anyone who was having difficulty and if she was needed, which was often the case, she was quite prepared to stay after hours to make sure you had grasped the problem.

Like most people, I've had my share of sadness and disappointments in life, but one of my saddest recollections, is of the time I had a chance meeting with this wonderful lady after leaving St. Anne's Primary. As I mentioned previously, I was employed by the Scottish Power Electricity Co. and I had to make a house call to take a meter reading at this certain address and it so happened that this house call was to become one of the most soul-destroying days that I'd had encountered in a very long time.

I arrived at the house and the name on the nameplate didn't register with me at all, until the lady opened the door and who should be standing there but Miss Melone. She hadn't really changed that much since I had first met her, but time seemed to have taken its toll as she was walking ever so slowly and she was stooped a little, but she was still very smartly dressed, as always, and never lost the appearance of a gracious lady. As I entered the house, I never thought for a moment that this woman would remember me, but I took the bold step of asking her if there was any chance that she did. She looked at me for a few seconds then inquired if I had been a pupil of hers at any time. I told her my surname and, before I had a chance to let her know my first name, she beat me to it. She proceeded to tell me that she also remembered teaching my sister Anne, who was three years younger than me. We then began to reminisce on old times and spoke about the former pupils she taught, asking if I ever came across any of them, considering the type of job I was doing. She also wanted to know that, if I ever met any of them, to please give them her best wishes.

I stayed stay for a little while longer as Miss Melone made me some tea, which was wonderful. We continued to talk over the old times at school, then came the bombshell. I asked her how she was getting on with her life and how she liked her retirement. She said she was doing alright and that her sister was now living with her, due to the fact that she had been diagnosed with having lung cancer. I was speechless. What do you say to a woman that you had come to admire and respect and all she had done for you education-wise? For the first time in years, I lost my composure and felt a lump in my throat. I was trying so hard to find the right words to say, but, true to form, she put me at ease. She must have noticed how I felt and began to tell me how she had been blessed by reaching a good age and how, as a young girl, she had always dreamed of becoming a teacher and got her wish by teaching all the young boys and girls. She said they were part of her one big family and it was her pleasure to have done this wonderful job.

It was time for me to go and it was, with profound sadness, that I took her hand in mine, gave her a tender hug and said my goodbyes. As I left her house, I walked down the street with tears in my eyes and, for the rest of that day, I couldn't get Miss Anna Melone out of my mind.

EPILOGUE

April 19, 1941 This was the day that I first opened my eyes to a world that was in the middle of a war which would last for another four years.

I was born in a house in Appin road, which was in the district of Dennistoun, and the reason for me being introduced to the devastation and deprivation of war from this part of the city, was because my father believed it would safer for my mother to stay with his brother's family than remain in their own home, in the East end of Glasgow, Bellfield street to be precise. I can only relate these facts as they were told to me by older members of my family who were there at the time to witness these scenes of decimation.

The German planes usually flew over the city at night time and frequently dropped their bombs along the Gallowgate as they made their way towards the Parkhead Forge. This was a large steel manufacturer which was producing steel for the war effort. So my father thought the best and safest course of action would be to send my mother to stay with relatives, while he remained to look after the rest of the family until things settled down. This turned out to be an act of providence, inasmuch as four days after my father had taken my mother to the safety of his relatives, a land mine, supposedly meant for the steel works, landed in the Speedwell Asphalt factory directly opposite our home. Needless to say, when this bomb exploded the building took the full blast, as no one expected an air raid that night. It was a miracle that there was only one fatality, as most people were at home. Rooftops were blown off, along with most of the windows and ceilings and, to add to the chaos, some families, who occupied the top flats, were virtually stranded, as staircases were collapsing cutting off their only way down.

The streets were littered with all sorts of obstacles, debris and glass, building rubble, electric cables from the telegraph poles, which had also collapsed and people, some in shock, wandered aimlessly, not even fully clothed, they were in pajamas, shirt and trousers, and some were even bare-footed. As this was all taking place, my father was trying to get our family together, this consisted of my brother James, sisters Martha, Mary and Lizzie. My father wanted to make sure everyone was safe and unhurt. Once he had established they were all unharmed, he was advised by an air raid warden to take them all down to a public school that was three streets away, there they were all given a blanket and cups of tea.

After seeing the rest of the family settled and safe, he then made his way to make sure that my mother and I had come to no harm. He stayed with us for a few hours and then returned back to the bomb damaged buildings and debris which, only a few days before, was Bellfield Street. He wanted to put his mind to rest that my brother and three sisters were being taken care of. Seeing all was well, he then made his way to our house to see if anything could be salvaged from our bomb ravaged home. However, he was not allowed to enter the building as it was declared unsafe by the A.R P. who had the authority to deem any bomb damaged building unsafe.

It took about four weeks before most of the houses were rendered safe to be occupied again. There were still those houses that still had to be renovated and the people who had occupied them previously were forced to stay in temporary accommodation such as schools and church halls, anywhere that could let these poor folk have a bed, meals and washing facilities.

For weeks on end, relatives were visiting these shelters looking for families and friends. Everything seemed to be quite chaotic, as people were coming and going, and there were no records of names of those who had been there. Lots of families were split up in the confusion following a bombing raid, and this added more worry to the parents and searchers, as they tried to establish where their loved ones could actually be. These events were all passed down to me from my brother, James, who had the misfortune to be part of this tragic time in his life. I, for my good fortune, can only remember vaguely the large bonfires that were lit in the street at the end of the war, when I must have been no more than four years of age and that was about a year before I started school.

What I can recall is the time I received my injury, what I still refer to as my own war wound. My older brother James was carrying me on top of his shoulders and happened to stumble, causing me to topple from his grasp and hit my forehead on the corner of a small, steel container that was filled with sand to douse any fires that were caused by the bombing. I still have the scar to this day, and, like most of the other boys and pals of mine, I collected more small marks and scars while growing up and playing in that wonderful place known universally as Glasgow.

I was actually raised and grew up in the Gallowgate, and that's where my best times were to be had. Playing moshie, kick-the-can, aleevio, jumping dykes, fitba'—it was a young boy's heaven. Even the lassies had great times playing wee shops, where they bought things with broken coloured glass that they would find on the ground in the backcourts. They enjoyed skipping ropes, and, as they were skipping, they would sing wee ditties in time with their jumping up and down.

Looking back to yesteryear, the Gallowgate that I knew was a district bursting with life, the sounds of the trams as they made their way towards the far reaching districts, or the carts that were always pulled by the large Clydesdale horses that made that wonderful clip, clop sound as their steel horseshoes landed on the cobbles.

These carts carried all sorts of wares, but I always liked to watch the cart that delivered the barrels of beer to the public house at the corner of our street. The cart would stop as the draymen unloaded the beer and that gave you the chance to go up close to these wonderful, docile, giant horses and give them a pat. The pavements always appeared to be teeming with throngs of people, mostly women, as they made their way to the shops, or returning home from their latest venture with their shopping bags laden with all sorts of goodies. The younger children zigzagging through the crowds as they chased one another, as their mother would be calling on them to stay close to her and to behave.

I can still see my old street and all the families who made the street what it was, the Duffys, Tobins, Herriots and Edwards, a full street comprising of nice folks, who would go out of their way to be helpful and, if they couldn't, they always knew someone who could, it was a type of real socialism that's rarely found in today's society.

Even the shopkeepers were a different breed, Sconie Johnnie, the baker, he made cakes and dumplings you would die for; Frank the Tally, the ice cream café owner; Moore the butcher, this is where all the housewives went at Hogmany to get their steak pie to lay out for visitors before the bells rang to herald in the New Year; the pawn shop which was called **Your Uncle John**. In fact, some of us were in it so often, he could have been a relative. I even had my first haircut in a famous barber shop that was part of the Gallowgate, the renowned Johnnie Ionta's. It was a small shop with only three chairs where you sat to get your hair cut, then there was also a short bench that held about four people where you would sit until it was your turn. Talking about turns, more often than not, while you were sitting waiting to get your haircut, there was always someone there playing the spoons or tap dancing or telling great jokes, so you didn't just get a haircut you were entertained as well.

Johnnie and his two brothers, Danny and Tommy, cut all the men's hair, then there was Agnes, who cut all the children's hair in the back of the shop. Every haircut that I ever got was done by Johnnie. My first haircut, so I've been told, was when I was three years old and that was in 1944 and my last haircut at Ionta's was in 1966, that's the year I got married. People came from all over Glasgow, and even further afield, came to get a haircut from the Ionta's shop. I've gone to get a haircut and couldn't get in the door owing to the fact there would be around twenty people all standing waiting in a queue.

I sometimes even came off the night shift and be at the shop before half past six in the morning, and there would be about seven people there before me, but it never bothered me to wait, because I would listen to Johnnie debating with Tommy and Danny about what had taken place the day before. It was hilarious to hear them as the patter was tremendous. The shop moved to the other side of the Gallowgate, next to the Bellgrove Hotel, but it was never quite the same as the old haunt.

Sadly, Johnnie passed away, but I shall always picture that wee man with the infectious laugh and his two brothers who brightened many a day for me.

Then, as my pals and I reached our later teens, we had the dancing to look forward to at the weekend. My first introduction to dancing took shape at St. Mary's church hall, where I would normally go on a Saturday night. This was a good place to learn with the rest of my friends from the guild, as we knew most of the girls who also went there. The only bugbear was that every now and then Canon Ward, who was the head priest in the chapel, would very often appear and stand at the door watching the dancers. He frowned upon anyone holding their partner too close, and he wasn't slow to let you know if it happened to be you. He gave you a look that could cut through steel as you danced passed him with the girl that you were holding, and you would adjust from holding her close to moving away from her, till she was at arm's length, and it appeared as if you were ballroom dancing.

It was an education to stand and study the couples who were really good dancers, it helped to watch them as they appeared to have the moves and steps down to a fine art. Then the next dance that you went to, you'd try to emulate the steps you saw from the previous dancers. This type of social hall was the place young people went to learn before progressing to the larger dance halls like Barrowland, where you could dance, or jive, to Billy McGregor's band, or the Dennistoun Palais, which had the Jack Anderston big band sound. Most nights, the dance halls were so busy you could stand in a queue for more than an hour before you gained entrance, and lots of folk met, not only a dance partner at the dancing, but their partner for life.

Dancing seemed to diminish as the discotheques began to take hold and the younger folk preferred this type of socializing, dancing to disc jockeys and pop groups and going to live concerts to see the most recent chart topping singer. Perhaps, dance halls shall make a comeback again, and the new, up-and-coming generation shall experience that wonderful feeling of holding a girl close as you glide across the floor, instead of standing gyrating, so far away from each other, that you have to use semaphore to communicate.

In getting that bit older, I now realize that things do change, but not always for the better, and I think it's a pity that the children I now see growing up, shall never experience the fun and good times that I shared with my pals in growing up in the old Glasgow tenements.

Sputtering Gas Lamps

Sentimentality and nostalgia are the back door to escapism from the here and now, returning you to the once-loved episodes of your life, to the happier times that were tested due to growing older and life-changing circumstances.

We stayed mid-landing in our tenement

Our close had some diverse characters. First, there was the "skipper" so named because he had been at sea most of his life and, upon his retirement, came to live with his sister. He was the first person I had ever seen wearing a morning gown. It was something to see him in his morning attire – gown, pyjamas, red slippers and a newspaper tucked under his arm along with his toilet roll. Whenever I happened to see him going for his ablutions, he would always say, "*Morning young laddie buck*" and, if you were waiting to get into the toilet, you had to wait until he read all the newspaper. So, it was a matter of good timing, or luck, to get in before him.

Then came the Bell family, who lived in the bottom flat, and you could tell when Mr. Bell came into the house all the worse for drink. He would open the window and throw Mrs. Bell's favourite photo of Pope Pius into the street, then all hell would break loose and, if any of Mrs. Bell's wishes come true, his arse will be roasting in hell this very minute.

Then there was old Dan McCulloch, who was around 80 years of age and a bit of a recluse. I believe he stayed at home most of the day, due to the fact that he had lost the use of his legs, and got around on two walking sticks. Now, whenever Dan did happen to venture out of the house, he would go down the stairs one at a time, so if you happened to be behind him, you had to wait until he had reached the top or the bottom, before you could pass. It had been known though, that if Dan had been making his way upstairs to his house and there were any of the girls who lived above him, he would stand to the side of the wall and allow the girl to hurry ahead of him. But, as she passed, Dan would use the tip of one of his sticks to lift the hemline of her dress, chuckle and say and "*Fine leg, lass.*" I can attest to that fact, as he did it to one of my sisters.

Another of Dan's quirks, was that he had a hatred for the sound of whistling. If he heard you whistle, he would shake his fist and curse and swear at you. I remember the time my brother,

Jimmy, and his pal, John Duffy, were walking down the stairs and Jimmy noticed Dan's door was half open. So, for devilment, Jimmy began whistling as loud as he could. Unlucky for John, he was in front of Jimmy and, as they passed old Dan's door, he brought one of his walking sticks down on John's head, laying him out for over ten minutes. John's mother contacted the police, but no action was taken against Dan. Another episode with Dan was the time he had a fall-out with the old lady, Mrs. Best, who lived directly below him. After a while, the fallout escalated into a full blown vendetta which ended when Dan tied a large iron onto the end of one of his sticks with a long piece of washing line, leaned out of his window and proceeded to smash all the window panes in her windows. This time, the police came and threw Dan into the Black Maria, followed by his two sticks. A few days later, the story appeared in the local press under the headlines *"She used to be Mrs. Best, now she's Mrs. Worst."* I don't recall ever seeing old Dan again after that incident and I believe no one else ever did.

There was also the street bookie, who sometimes would stand at the back of the close and take bets from all and sundry, for horse and dog racing. People soon got to know where he stood at certain times of the day, so they would make their way to that part of the street to lay their bets. The bookie would usually stay in that close for a few weeks and then move to another part of the street, because as street gambling was illegal, he would do his best to avoid the police, so moving around was his best bet, *"If you'll pardon the pun."*

Most bookies usually did their business in the back closes, but there was one bookie who took bets inside his house, so he was never suspected of taking bets from the public. But, as time wore on, some other bookies began renting small shops, setting up a telephone relay to the tracks and take bets in the shop. In this way, they attracted more punters as they could see the odds and even prices on a large blackboard and, as the betting prices were coming straight from the track, they saw the betting prices fluctuate at first hand. More often than not, these shops would be raided by the police, but the bookie always seemed to know in advance the exact date and time when he was going to be turned over, this was mostly due to the fact that some of the beat police, who would usually stop in at these premises and get a cup of tea, or something a bit stronger, would forewarn him of the raid. The bookie would then get some of his usual punters to be in the shop and give them all ten shillings each. Come the raid, they would all be arrested, appear in court, and the bookie paid all of their fines. This system worked out well, because the punters got their few shillings for just being there, so they were quite happy, but if there had been a raid without the bookie knowing, all the takings would have been confiscated. In this way, it gave the bookie the opportunity to get most of the money out of the way, and leaving some money in the cash box before the police showed up, So everyone was a winner, the punter got a few bob, it saved the bookie a bit of cash, and the polis' still got their cup of tea, or something stronger.

Talking of gambling, my mind goes back to the time that my uncle Frank had a greyhound that was named Tina. Uncle Frank had great hopes for this dog and believed that he had a good chance of Tina being a winner. This being said, he took the dog to a track where they would time the dog over a certain distance, but the night he took the dog was the night that they usually timed the dogs jumping over hurdles, Tina had never jumped prior to this, so Uncle Frank was jumping over the hurdle first and then Tina would follow. So, after doing a full lap of the track, the man who was timing the dogs and watching how well they jumped, said to Uncle Frank *"The dog just won't do, but the good news is we can enter you for the second race this Saturday."*

Playing fitba' in the street was always one of my favourite pastimes and I shall forever carry the fond memories of the street games. Every street had a team made up from all the boys who lived there. All the street teams had their own name, all my pals who played in our team adopted the name "**The Bellfield Runners**" which was really quite appropriate, as most of the time we always seemed to be running away from the polis' who took a dim view of anyone playing fitba' in the street.

We would play other street teams from all over the Gallowgate and even some teams from farther afield. Some of the games lasted for hours and even when the light began to fade, we would keep on playing under the street lamps until it was nearly virtually impossible to see the ball, then we would have to call it a day, because you started to miss the ball and make contact with some poor guys leg, it got to the stage that you were going home with your legs covered in bruises. We would then arrange a rematch for a certain day at the other team's street and this went on all summer, as long as we had good weather to continue our games.

The Hearse:

"*Hey Alex, you can blaw a bugle can't ye'?*" "*Aye*" I replied, "*but whit dae ye' want tae know that for?*" "*Oh nuthin', ah just wondered*" he mumbled. Nothing, he said, but I knew better, it wasn't like my brother Jimmy to ask questions for nothing, there must have been some sort of reason for him to be asking. Yes, I could blow a bugle, that is, I could blow one very loud, but as for playing any sort of tune, that I couldn't do. The old bugle that I used to blow belonged to my father, who happened to be a bugler in the First World War with his regiment **The Royal Scots,** and after the war had ended, he brought his bugle back home as a souvenir.

I used to play with this bugle at home. When I was younger, I would often take it out of the house whenever my pals were playing cowboys and Indians and pretend to be in the cavalry, leading the charge, blowing the bugle and making one hell of a racket.

It had been a good few years since I had seen this bugle and had forgotten all about it and that's what got me puzzled, why I was being asked if I could blow one. A few days, later the puzzle was solved. I had just come into the house from school, changed into my old clothes, ready to go out and play for a few hours before supper, when who should walk in the door, but Jimmy and my brother-in-law, Tommy. *"Ah! Just the man we want tae see. We've just bought somethin' that's gonnae make us a right few bob an' you can be in the money, as well as us, if ye' want tae get involved."* Before I could answer, Jimmy said *"C'mon doon tae the street an we'll show ye."* So down the stairs we trooped and, when we got to the street, I asked *"Well, whit did ye' buy that's gonnae make ye' rich?"* *"That,"* says Tommy, pointing over to the other side of the street. I couldn't believe my eyes, there it stood, a large black hearse that they had bought down at the car auctions. It had all the trimmings, long windows that let you see the coffin as it lay on top of these silver rods, silver wheel covers and small black curtains that could be drawn across the windows.

For a few seconds, I could picture Jimmy and Tommy sitting up front driving this monstrosity and that was enough to get me started, I began laughing and just couldn't stop, every time I thought of the two of them sitting in this hearse, it would set me off again. Just then, who should turn up but Paddy Tobin, one of the boys who lived up our close. *"Whit's aw the laughin' aboot, is somebody tellin' dirty jokes?"* he asked. When I explained to Paddy about why I was laughing and what they had bought, he said *"Ah suppose yer goin' intae the boady snatchin' or takin'up undertakin'? Noo mind whit yer lettin' yersel' intae fer it's a dyin' trade!"* With that parting advice, he walked away laughing just as hard as I had been.

Once we all went back up to the house, Jimmy said *"Tae let ye' understaun' we're gonnae huv a go at the toys-fer-rags gemme. There's good money tae be made aff the woollens an' any o' the big rag stores take them aff yer haunds fer a fair bit o' cash."* *"Aye, well just keep yer haunds aff ma clobber. if any o' mah woollen jumpers or socks go missin' ah'll know who tae blame."* I said, before once more going into fits of laughter. *"O.K. laugh aw ye want, but when we're rollin' in the money we'll huv the last laugh"* said Tommy. *"Aye maybe so, but if ye' see me in the street when ye're oot drivin' yer hearse, without a boady, lookin' as if yer lost, an' searchin' fer wan, don't bother tae gie' me a wave, people might think ah'm helpin' ye oot"*

"By the way" Jimmy pipes up *"talkin' aboot helpin' oot, how wid ye' like tae?"* *"Stoap right there"* I said, as the penny had suddenly dropped. *"There's no way in God's green earth that ah'm gonnae sit in a coffin carrier, blawin' a bugle tae attract weans tae bring oot old rags."* *"Haud oan a wee minute noo, ye' widdnae be daen this free gratis"* he said. *"We'll gie ye two pounds an mebbe even a bit mair, dependin' on how well we dae. So you'll make a few bob just fer blawin' a bugle."* *"Naw, no way will ye' get me sittin' in a bloody great hearse, whit if any o' mah pals see me, ah'd never live it doon. It wid spread aw' ower the place, ah can see it noo, Alex leadin' the ragmen's charge."* *"Look"* says Jimmy, *"here's whit we'll dae. Ye can sit up front wi' Tommy an' me an' when we get a good wee pile o' rags, ye can then go intae the back, blaw the bugle oot the windae an' then lie under the rags. That way naebody will see ye. At least, gie it a try."* *"Naw"* I said *"an' ah mean **naw**."*

Well, came the Saturday and there I was, sitting up front with the two entrepreneurs and, to be truthful, they were doing alright, as far as getting plenty of rags was concerned. It was really something to watch two grown men bartering with boys and girls as to what type of toy they could get for the amount of rags that they brought to the hearse. Sometimes the kid's mother would come and complain about what her child got. As far as I was concerned, that was the bosses worry, I was just there to blow the bugle.

We were in a housing scheme named Castlemilk, which was a far cry from where we lived, so as I knew no one from that district, I was becoming quite confident and, by this time I was in the back of the hearse, opening the small window and blowing the bugle for all I was worth, which was the princely sum of two pounds. After a while, we stopped for a bite to eat and Jimmy and Tommy went into the back of the motor to separate the woollens from the rest of the cloth. "*Hey! Look at this.*" Tommy had been at the back going through the rags and, on turning some over, discovered a nearly new Crombie coat. This type of coat was all the rage at the time and was really quite expensive, how it came about ending up amongst the rags, was a mystery. "*It must huv been thrown in the back wi' a bundle o' rags*" said Tommy "*the thing is how dae we find oot who belongs tae it. We cannae go back roon aw the doors asking people is it theirs, any bugger could claim it. Naw, ah think the best idea is tae keep it fer ourselves, but ah'll tell ye this, if we get it dry-cleaned, we'll get a right few bob fer it.*" "*Sounds good,*" said Jimmy "*but let's get tae hell oot o' here just in case somebody does comes lookin' fer it.*"

So we made off to our next port of call, which was another housing scheme, known as Cranhill. I wasn't looking forward to going there, because my sister Lizzie and her family had lived there for a good many years and I was up there quite a lot, between going to the disco in the small community hall and sometimes playing football with the local team, the Springboig YMCA, so I had got to know lots of the people from there. So now my next course of action was to stay in the back of the hearse, hide under the rags then, every so often, pop up, blow the bugle, then duck out of sight under the rags again before I was noticed by anyone who knew me.

Everything was going to plan, then disaster. I suddenly popped up from lying prostrate to blow the bugle through the small window, but it was really bad timing, because the hearse stopped just as an elderly couple were standing at the kerb waiting to cross the road. I was within touching distance of these old people and, as I looked straight into the face of the old lady, I swear I thought she was going to have a heart attack. I don't know who got the biggest fright, her or me. Although I don't think I shall ever see such a look of shock on any ones face again. After a few Saturdays, I gave up my career as a ragman's bugle boy, but I'll never have the thrill again of getting a sore throat and saggy cheeks, all that and two pounds appearance money.

So now to attract the children, Jimmy and Tommy got themselves a large bell, but it was money down the drain, because the old hearse had seen its day and had to be scrapped. That was shortly after I had stopped going with them. But I remember the night Jimmy told me they had to get rid of the motor because the engine was dead, so again I couldn't help laughing as I told him they should get a hearse to take it to the nearest cemetery. As I ran out the front door, the book that he had been reading came whistling past my head. It didn't all turn out too bad though, because they got the Crombie coat cleaned and took turns at wearing it, whenever the occasion arose.

Street entertainers

There was also the street and backcourt entertainment. In the hot, drawn out summer evenings, you would often get a visit from Matt Bonn and his two sidekicks. Matt would play the accordion and one of his mates would imitate Charlie Chaplin. He would dress up like Charlie and do the funny walk and, as Matt played some tunes, his other pal would tap-dance. After a short performance, Matt would go around the small crowd that had gathered and collect some money in a hat, before moving onto the next street. Then there was a large, thin man who pushed a pram with an old wind-up gramophone inside. The boys from the street christened him "**Jasper**." He stood well over six feet tall and wore a coat and tails and he always had a tile hat on his head, he did his act in the backcourts of the streets and had the deepest voice that you could ever imagine. His repertoire consisted of hymns, which he sang with his deep, gravely voice and, after finishing a hymn, he would wind up the old gramophone and play an old scratchy record as he went around picking up the few coppers or sometimes even a slice of bread or a piece of fruit that had been wrapped in paper.

I don't know whether the people who threw these rewards from their windows was to show their appreciation, or to get him to take his pram and voice elsewhere to escape the din. Although I don't think Jasper cared, because he was earning some money and, at the same time, keeping hunger at bay.

There was one Saturday afternoon, when he was singing one of his favourite hymns, "**Faith of our Fathers.**" This happened to be a hymn that my mother liked to hear and it must have made her feel charitable. When Jasper noticed my Mother raising the window, he stood underneath waiting for his reward for his fine rendition of the song. There were a few apples on the table, so picking one up, my Mother dropped it into his hands, he, in turn, dropped it onto the ground, then looking up, as if to say *"I can't eat that now because it fell on the ground"* my mother threw down another apple, so, quick as a flash, Jasper caught the second one, picked up the first one from the ground, grabbed the pram and moved to the next backcourt. Now that's what you call living by your wits.

Even when you were standing in a queue waiting to get in to see a movie, sure as fate, someone would show up and do an act, whether it was to sing or dance, just to make a few shillings. You don't seem to get this type of thing anymore, perhaps it's the affluent society we now live in, or maybe it's because there's no more backcourts or cinema queues.

Frankie Vaughn:

In the early 60s, the gang culture, which had plagued Glasgow for years, had returned. One of the prime reasons for the upsurge of violence to rear its ugly head once more, in my mind, was mainly due to the fact that the powers that be had seen fit to demolish the inner city houses. Houses that could, and should have been renovated were demolished and, in their place, housing schemes were built on the outskirts of the city. So, in one fell swoop, not only did they remove the streets, they decimated communities. The Castlemilk housing scheme was built in the 50s with no thought, whatsoever, for the young people, or even the older members of the families who were placed in these barren, isolated, out of the way, concrete housing schemes.

There were no shops, schools, youth clubs, swimming baths, absolutely nothing for the teenage youths, so if they wanted to go to a dance or a disco, see a movie, or even purchase some clothing, they would have to travel into the city. There wasn't even a public house in the area and it was known as a dry zone until the 80s, when a pub, which shall remain unnamed, was allowed to open. I was told by a friend of mine who lived in the district, that at the start it was a good safe place to go for a quiet drink, but, as usual, after a few weeks it became the haunt of the unsavoury characters and became a rather rough and ready place, prone to the occasional donnybrook.

It got to the stage that it was now known as a very unsavoury establishment. He also told me that one rainy evening, which is most unusual in Glasgow, as he was passing this pub with his pal, they noticed seven men sitting on a wall, outside the pub, nonchalantly drinking pints of beer as the rain drizzled down on them. When asked why were sitting in the rain, his pal said "*Oh them, they're barred*" meaning they couldn't go inside for a pint. So even the grown ups, who wanted to have a night out with their wife or friends, had to go into the city. Now, due to the isolation and the lack of amenities, all that was left for the young folk was to wander around in groups at night and into other parts of the estate. This, in turn, led to other groups of young people becoming territorial, so if any other boys came into their patch there was always going to be bad blood between different factions, escalating into gang problems.

This had been allowed to fester for many years and there seemed to be no way to stop the violence. Young men were being badly injured and even fatal stabbings were becoming the norm. This was a problem that was affecting all the large housing schemes and the gang culture was escalating.

I remember the time that Frankie Vaughn came to Glasgow. He said that, in his younger days, he was a member of a gang from Liverpool called "**The Dingle Boys**" so he thought it might be a nice gesture if he could get most of the gangs, from different districts, together and talk to them about the futility of being a gang member.

His first visit was to the Calton district which was where the **"Calton Tongs"** were the local gang. As is usual, the media got wind of this and the next thing you knew the newspapers were getting in on the act. The police said that there would be an amnesty and no questions would be asked whenever you handed in a weapon. So they got a few large oil drums and the objective was that they could bring along the weapon and it would be dropped into the oil drum. Now, we had Frankie, the police and the newspaper photographers all ready and waiting for the show to begin. For a start, everybody wanted in on the act and get their photo in the newspaper, standing beside Frankie Vaughn.

The whole thing ended up being a fiasco, young people, some as young as 14 years old, were handing in all sorts of things, knives, chisels, iron bars, hammers, you name it and it was there. The place was mobbed, all the young girls, even some not so young, wanted to see Frankie Vaughn the star, but it was later stated that mothers couldn't lay their hands on a knife for days, the kids had taken them and dropped them into the oil drum, hoping to maybe get their photo in the newspaper.

The next day, Frankie said that the amnesty was a huge success, although I imagine he may have changed his view a few days later when he visited the Easterhouse scheme, where he gave the same talk to the local badlads. When it was time to leave, he discovered someone had stolen his overcoat, perhaps someone had taken it for a souvenir. But fair play to Mr. Frankie Vaughn, he gave a concert at the Glasgow Pavilion and donated the proceeds to the Easterhouse Project. Sadly, Frankie passed away aged 71 in 1999, but his legacy is still going strong.